Nuts
PUB
AMMO

THIS IS A CARLTON BOOK

Published by The Carlton Publishing Group
20 Mortimer Street
London W1T 3JW

ISBN 978-1-78097-436-1

10 9 8 7 6 5 4 3 2

Printed and bound by CPI Group (UK) Ltd, Croydon, CR0 4YY

Nuts
PUB
AMMO

CARLTON
BOOKS

A message from
THE Nuts TEAM

Simply by buying *Nuts Pub Ammo*, you have
revealed that you are a being of considerable
intelligence. In many ways, the very fact that
you are smart enough to have bought it means
that you have scant need for the nuggets of
information nestling within. But you can never
know too much stuff. And that's what this book
is about. It's about knowing stuff. Lots of stuff.
Over the past two-and-a-half years, the Pub
Ammo page in *Nuts* magazine has accumulated
many, many astounding facts. Did you know, for
example, that a hippo's lips are two feet wide?
Now you do. That's just one of the thousands
of facts you can find in this book, facts that you
can store in your mind and then impart to your
mates in the pub, or perhaps use to impress a
lady. Because that's what facts are for.
Read on, wise *Nuts* person, and fill your head
with incredible stuff!

* The genetic make-up of a human is 57 per cent the same as that of a cabbage.

* A "jiffy" is an actual unit of time equal to 1/100th of a second.

* Residents of Hawaii eat an average of four cans of Spam per person, per year – more than in any other place on Earth.

The quickest boxing match in history was 10.5 seconds. This included the 10-second count.

* A Saudi Arabian woman can file for divorce if her husband doesn't make her a cup of coffee.

* Men are four times more likely to be struck by lightning than women.

* **The average duration of sexual intercourse for humans is two minutes.**

* In 1980, the Yellow Pages accidentally listed a Texas funeral home under "frozen foods".

* **The number of Britons injured last year in accidents involving out-of-control Scalextric cars was five.**

The most common name for a pub in England is The Red Lion.

* During George W Bush's recent state visit to Britain, muggings went up by 20 per cent.

* **By law, every child in Belgium must take harmonica lessons.**

* *The Goodies* is the only British comedy said to have killed someone. On 24 March 1975, bricklayer Alex Mitchell, of King's Lynn,

apparently laughed himself to death while watching a sketch about a Scotsman being attacked by a black pudding.

* **The thickest skin on humans is on the upper back and weighs 3.2kg in total. The thinnest skin is on the eyelids.**

* When you lick a stamp, you take in one calorie.

* **Roughly 120 million acts of sexual intercourse occur every day.**

* When dying, seeing is the first sense to go.

The average human eats eight spiders during his or her lifetime.

* **Pearls melt in vinegar.**

* The most disastrous war for any country in history was Paraguay's war against Argentina, Brazil and Peru of 1864-1870,

which reduced the country's population from 1.3m to 221,000. Paraguay started it.

✳ **The longest word in the English language has 1,909 letters and refers to DNA.**

✳ The penguin is the only bird that walks upright. It's also the only bird that can swim but can't fly.

✳ **Every day, 20 banks are robbed.**

✳ China has more English speakers than the United States.

✳ **There isn't a single reference to a cat in the Bible.**

Carrots were originally purple. The Dutch bred orange carrots in the 17th century, which proved more popular.

* In space it is impossible to cry – the tears cannot run because of the lack of gravity.

* **Mother tarantulas kill 99 per cent of the babies they hatch.**

* Disneyworld is bigger than the world's five smallest countries.

The blue whale has a heart the size of a small car and its blood vessels are so broad that a person could swim through them.

* **Women blink nearly twice as much as blokes, although the figure for lesbians is closer to men.**

* Saudi Arabia has no natural rivers.

* **The giant telescope on Mount Palomar, California, can see a distance of 7,038,835,200,000,000,000,000 miles.**

* 80-85 per cent of men who die from heart attacks during intercourse are found to have been cheating on their wives.

* **With the equivalent fuel load to a jumbo jet, a car could drive around the world four times.**

* Ian "Lovejoy" McShane turned down the chance to play for Manchester United in order to concentrate on acting.

14-year-old Annika Irmler, from Tangstedt, near Hamburg, has the longest tongue in the world – 2.75 inches.

* **Indian doctors were performing plastic surgery and fitting fake limbs 2,600 years ago.**

* Some species of shark can grow, lose and regrow as many as 30,000 teeth in their lifetime.

✳ **From 1600 to 1680, 40,000 people were burned to death for witchcraft in Britain.**

✳ So far, 119 planets have been identified outside the solar system.

✳ **Albania has the lowest suicide rate in Europe.**

The British brought the world the bicycle, the refrigerator and the war tank. The French brought us the tie, the handkerchief and wallpaper.

✳ More than 75 per cent of Australia is considered to be "the outback".

✳ **Tarantulas do not leave any tracks on sand.**

✳ In Alexandria, Minnesota, it's illegal for a man to have sex if he has garlic, onions or sardines on his breath.

* **The Eiffel Tower weighs 10,100 tonnes.**

* In 1961, the Brazilian government passed a law banning the sale of Pele to an overseas club.

> The badminton shuttlecock is the second-fastest object in sport, after the ball in Jai-Alai, an obscure Basque game. It regularly travels at 110mph and has clocked up to 180mph.

* **Between 1991 and 2003, attempted bank robberies in Britain fell from 1,400 a year to 250.**

* Threadneedle Street in the City of London used to be called Gropecunte Lane.

* **Dolphins have two brains and never sleep with both at once.**

* Tony Blair is an honorary member of the Dennis the Menace fan club.

* **One in ten adults has an extra pair of ribs.**

* Vesna Vulovic holds the record for the longest fall without a parachute. The Serbian air stewardess was on board a JAT flight that was blown up in mid-air on 26 January 1972, and fell 33,000 ft. She survived.

* **Less than 50 people have ever reached the age of 114, only 20 have made it to 115 and six have hit 116. Jeanne Louise Calment of France was the oldest person in history, living from 21 February 1875 to 4 August 1997 – 122 years. Sadly, in 1996 she released a rap album, _Time's Mistress_.**

If you upset a hippo, its sweat turns red.

* MPs are forbidden from putting their hands in their pockets while in the House of Commons. Likewise, no reading material, medals or hats can be worn.

* **Walsall is the fattest town in Britain.**

* The Bible is the most shoplifted book in America.

```
There are at least 92
nuclear bombs lost in the
sea somewhere.
```

* **In *The Last Temptation Of Christ*, you can see the label in Christ's robe.**

* If you deprive a goldfish of light, it will eventually turn almost white.

* **Most toilets flush in the key of E-flat.**

* The world's first restaurant was opened in Kaifeng, China in 1153. It is still operating.

* **The tin can was invented in 1810 – the can opener in 1858. For those 48 years in between, a hammer and chisel were used.**

* An error in the 1631 King James Bible left the 7th commandment as "Thou shalt commit adultery". Though they were recalled and most destroyed (and the printer fined the equivalent of £250), 11 still remain.

* **Lake Karachay in Western Siberia is officially the most polluted place on earth, according to the Worldwatch Institute.**

* The second man to play James Bond in any medium was Bob Holness of *Blockbusters* fame, starring in a 1957 South African radio dramatisation of *Moonraker*.

This year, the rat population in the UK will overtake the human population for the first time.

* **Roman Polanski's 1971 film *Macbeth* featured none other than Keith Chegwin.**

* Australia is the serious assault capital of the world, notching up 708 per 100,000 people in 1999. Even Rwanda, three years after its genocide, managed only 114.

* **Antony Worrall Thompson's fingers are insured for £1million.**

* The Earth experiences 50,000 earthquakes each year.

* **10,000 people in the UK pick the numbers 1 to 6 in the weekly lottery.**

* Adamnan the Viking was the first person to see the Loch Ness Monster, in 565.

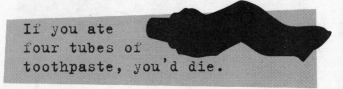

If you ate four tubes of toothpaste, you'd die.

* **The bar tally for Oliver Reed's last bender was eight lagers, 12 double rums and half a bottle of whisky.**

* A total of $1trillion in US armaments are missing, including 56 whole warplanes, 32 tanks and 36 javelin missiles.

* **In the 16th century in Holland, Spain and England, urine was used as a tooth-cleaning agent by, among others, Queen Elizabeth I.**

Every month, Thames Water filters a ton of pubic hair from treatment sites. The pubes are buried as landfill.

* Jerome Irving Rodale, founder of the organic food movement, boasted on *The Dick Cavett Show* in January 1971: "I'm going to live to be 100 unless I'm run down by a sugar-crazed taxi driver." Minutes later, he dropped dead after having a heart attack.

* **The British–Zanzibar war of 1896 is the shortest war in the history books – Zanzibar surrendered after 38 minutes.**

* British stamps are the only ones that don't state the country of origin, as this was the first country to issue them, back in 1840.

* **Until late medieval times, little girls were traditionally clothed in black rather than pink, while sky blue for boys was designated to seek the assistance of the pre-Christian sky gods (Thor, Zeus and Jupiter).**

There are more guns in Switzerland (eight million) than there are people (seven-and-a-half million).

* The shortest scheduled flight in the world is between Westray and Papa Westray in the Orkneys, lasting two minutes.

* **The word "Mafia" was never used in *The Godfather*.**

* The full name of Los Angeles is "El Pueblo de Nuestra Señora la Reina de los Angeles de Porciúncula".

* **A pig's orgasm lasts for 30 minutes.**

* The metal bit at the top of a pencil that holds the rubber in is called a ferrule.

* **Ainsley Harriott was a gelf in *Red Dwarf*.**

* Hull City is the only British league football team whose name doesn't have any letters you can colour in.

* **In Monopoly, you are statistically more likely to land on Trafalgar Square than any other square.**

* The microwave was invented when a scientist walked past a radar tube with a bar of chocolate in his pocket and it melted.

More than half of all residents of Arkansas swear they have seen a UFO.

* You are 139 times more likely to die in the car on the way to the airport than you are flying in the plane.

* Americans eat about 18 acres of pizza a day.

* Since DNA evidence became legally acceptable, 75 death-row prisoners in America have been cleared of the crimes they were sentenced for.

* *Apollo 14* astronaut Alan Shepard holds the record for the longest golf drive ever (2,400ft). He was on the moon when he teed off.

```
A hippo can hold its breath
underwater for five minutes.
A beaver can hold its breath
underwater for 15 minutes.
```

* More than 100 women make their living by impersonating Marilyn Monroe.

* Rotten wood will glow in the dark.

* If Silicon Valley in California, USA, were to declare independence, it would be counted as the world's fifth-largest economy.

Plump game bird the pheasant originates from China.

* You can write 50,000 words with a single HB pencil.

* In 1555, Ivan the Terrible had the architects of St Basil's Church in Moscow blinded so they would never be able to design anything as beautiful.

* Verkhoyansk, Siberia, has the most extremely varying climate in the world, with temperatures ranging from a low of -68°C in the winter to a high of 37°C in the summer.

* The smallest country in the world is the Sovereign Military Republic of Malta, which occupies a single room in a building in Rome.

＊There are more species of butterfly to be found in a square mile of tropical rainforest than there are in the entire North American continent.

＊**The world's largest collection of human brains (8,000) is kept beneath the Runwell Psychiatric Hospital in Essex.**

```
You're more likely to be
killed by a rogue champagne
cork than a poisonous
spider bite.
```

＊The cracks in breaking glass move at speeds of up to 3,000mph.

＊**There are 17 species of walnut.**

＊The world's widest highway is the Monumental Axis in the Brazilian capital, Brasilia, where 160 cars can drive side by side.

Last year, doctors in Vienna performed the first ever human tongue transplant.

* Anfield's Kop was named after a battle in the Boer War on 23 January 1900 on a hill known as Spioenkop, meaning "spy hill" in Afrikaans. Three hundred British soldiers were killed, many of them coming from Merseyside.

* If two flies were able to reproduce in a controlled environment without predators for a year, the resulting mass of insect offspring would be the size of Earth.

* One in eight US workers have, at some point, worked the grill in McDonald's.

* An estimated 100,000 birds die each year by flying kamikaze into the McCormick Plaza in Chicago.

* Beer mat collectors are officially known as tegestologists.

* There are no houses numbered 1 to 9 on Downing Street.

* **According to the National Criminal Intelligence Service, there are 930 "families" of gangsters in the UK with a combined turnover of £50billion per year.**

```
Elvis had a twin brother, named
Jesse, who died at birth.
```

* Since the '70s, microchips have doubled in power and halved in price every two years.

* **World War II was the first conflict in history where a soldier had more chance of being killed in combat than by disease.**

* The Congo River is also called the Zaire River.

* **Indian restaurants in the UK now employ more people than the mining and shipbuilding industries combined.**

There is a model of
Superman somewhere in
all 180 episodes of US
sitcom Seinfeld.

* The Atacama Desert is the
  driest in the world — some parts
  haven't experienced rainfall in 500 years
  of recorded history.

* **There's an annual Rock, Paper, Scissors
  world tournament held in Koolhaus,
  Toronto. The winner gets $3,750.**

* A "tin" can is actually made out of steel,
  with an anti-rust coating of tin that's just
  0.0005mm thick.

* **Ray Kroc, the founder of McDonald's, and
  Walt Disney were in the same WWI Army
  unit.**

* The Earth is hit by lightning over 100 times
  a second.

* Statistically speaking, during a football match, it is worth being sent off for committing a professional foul which prevents a goal being scored – but only after at least 16 minutes of the game have been played.

A squirrel cannot contract or carry the rabies virus.

* The average American is filmed on closed-circuit cameras seven times a day.

* The longest skid by a car was made by Simon de Banke, who maintained a controlled power slide in a Subaru Impreza for more than 2hrs 11mins.

* The faeces of Italian artist Piero Manzoni were sold at auction for $75,000.

* Americans eat approximately ten billion doughnuts annually – not each.

* F1 ace Jenson Button failed his driving test first time around.

* **Libra (the scales) is the only inanimate symbol in the zodiac.**

* The biggest sumo wrestler in the world is Hawaiian-born Akebono. He weighs in at 501lb and stands 6ft 8ins tall.

* **The longest movie ever made is *The Cure For Insomnia* (1987), which clocks in at 85 hours.**

* The Main Library at Indiana University sinks over an inch every year because, when it was built, engineers failed to take into account the increasing weight of all the books in the building.

You have a one in 10 trillion chance of being hit by a meteor.

* If you stay awake for 17 hours, you will suffer a decrease in physical performance equivalent to a blood alcohol level of 0.05 per cent.

* The wingspan of a Boeing 747 is longer than the Wright brothers' very first flight.

* Just 20 seconds of fuel remained when *Apollo 11*'s lunar module landed on the moon.

In March 2004, an asteroid buzzed the Earth at some 43,000 kilometres, the closest recorded miss ever.

* A lion's roar can be heard from up to five miles away.

* German chemists have made a replica of the World Cup trophy that is the size of one molecule. That is less than 100-millionth the size of the original.

* Shakespeare invented more than 2,000 words, including "assassination" and "bump".

* It is estimated that, at any one time, 0.7 per cent of the world's population is drunk.

* A whopping $26billion in ransom payments have been paid out in the US over the past 20 years.

* You share your birthday with at least nine million other people in the world.

* Hitler was claustrophobic. The lift leading to his Eagle's Nest hideout in the Austrian Alps was mirrored so it would appear larger and more open.

* There is a church in Spain that allows worshippers to make donations via a credit card terminal.

Until 1997, there were more pigs than people in Denmark.

* Mosquito repellents don't repel them – instead, they hide you. The spray blocks the mosquito's sensors so they don't know you're there.

* **0.3 per cent of all road accidents in Canada involve a moose.**

* The length of the finger dictates how fast the fingernail grows. Therefore, the nail on your middle finger grows the fastest and, on average, your toenails grow half as quickly as your fingernails.

* **One in three Americans carries a handgun in their car.**

* Any free-moving liquid in outer space will form itself into a sphere, because of its surface tension.

* **Your stomach needs to produce a new layer of mucus every two weeks or it would digest itself.**

* Mexico City boasts the world's largest taxi fleet. The capital has over 60,000 cabs.

* **If you go blind in one eye you only lose about one fifth of your vision but all your sense of depth.**

* In ancient Rome, it was considered a sign of leadership to be born with a crooked nose.

```
Rattlesnakes can swim and
bite underwater.
```

* **After a road traffic collision, traffic backs up at a rate of a mile every minute.**

* Canada is the only country not to win a gold medal in the summer Olympic Games while hosting the event.

* The "rusticles" on the model of the sunken *Titanic* in the film were bran flakes painted with rust-coloured paint.

* There's a place in France called "Y".

* Jeremy Bentham, a British philosopher who died in 1832, left his entire estate to the London Hospital, provided his body be allowed to preside over its board meetings. His skeleton was clothed and fitted with a wax mask of his face. It was present at the meeting for 92 years.

```
The human heart produces enough
pressure to squirt blood nine
metres.
```

* Each of us generates about 3.5lb of trash a day. Most of it is paper.

* Jars of peanut butter are the items most often mistaken for explosives by airport scanners.

180 workers died during the making of the Mount Rushmore landmark.

* Today's mobile phones use more digital technology than the spacecraft which put man on the moon.

* **Snooker balls are made by pouring composite resins into the casings of light bulbs.**

* Greece's national anthem has no fewer than 158 verses.

* **The street address of the White House is 1600 Pennsylvania Avenue.**

* The biggest ever win on a fruit machine was £21.6million in Las Vegas, in 2003.

* **72 per cent of women admit to being attracted to the bad guy in a movie.**

* In the Great Fire of 1666, half of London was destroyed, but only six people were killed.

The time taken to reduce the
average adult corpse to ashes
during cremation is an hour
and a half.

* **200 people are injured every year when
  their collapsible bikes... collapse.**

* Viagra was discovered by accident. Scientists
  were actually trying to come up with a
  treatment for angina.

* **The only two sterile natural environments
  on Earth are the centre of the Atacama
  Desert and the craters of erupting
  volcanoes.**

* The largest combined serving of fish and
  chips weighed 12.72kg. The fish weighed
  6.06kg and the chips 6.66kg.

* **Subbuteo world champion Massimiliano
  Natasi has his flicking finger insured
  for £31,000.**

* Rhino horn sells for £650 per kilo on the market. The poachers who collect it are paid £45 a week.

* **Out of the 23,000 Japanese soldiers who died during the battle for Guadalcanal in World War II, only ten per cent died from bullets. The rest died from fever, malaria and hunger.**

* The human memory is equivalent to 1,048,576 megabytes.

* **The guest commentator for Italian TV's coverage of the recent Sampdoria vs Juventus game was the Archbishop of Genoa, Cardinal Tarcisio Bertone. He left early to take mass.**

```
In 1991, the average
bra size in the US
was a 34B. Today,
it's a 36C.
```

* The greatest height from which an egg has been dropped to Earth without breaking is 213m.

* **It is impossible to retrieve anything deleted from a mobile phone.**

Scorpions are not immune to their own poison.

* ET's face was an amalgam of Albert Einstein, poet Carl Sandburg and a pug dog.

* **At full speed, a cheetah takes strides of eight metres.**

* The desert-dwelling kangaroo rat never has to drink water – it can metabolise it from food.

* **Human blood travels 60,000 miles per day on its journey through the body.**

* The opening to the cave in which a bear hibernates is always on the north slope of a hill.

* **King Charles I's head was sewn back on to his body after his execution so that his portrait could be painted.**

* Nutmeg is extremely poisonous if injected intravenously.

* **According to the National Earthquake Information Centre, 18 major earthquakes occur each year around the world.**

```
There are more than 700 pieces
of space debris — ranging from
pebble size to objects as
large as buses — orbiting the
earth.
```

* The first product to be purchased by scanning its barcode was a single pack of chewing gum.

> A rat can lift 116 per cent of its own body weight.

* Twelve astronauts have walked on the moon.

* In July 1942, US dollar bills for circulation in Hawaii had the name of the island printed on them to keep the money isolated from the rest of the US, in case Japan invaded Hawaii.

* There are 193 countries in the world, 61 dependent areas, and six disputed territories.

* The first recorded hijacking of an aeroplane took place on 21 February 1931, when a group of rebel soldiers in Peru forced two American pilots to fly them over Lima and drop propaganda.

* The biggest registered tip of £23,000 was given to a dancer at Stringfellows.

* The drugs used in lethal injections are a combination of sodium pentothal, pavulon and potassium chloride.

* **At one point, OJ Simpson was considered for the lead role in *The Terminator*.**

```
The world's largest ever
cup of coffee measured
2,500 litres.
```

* An iPod Nano has a million times more storage than the on-board computer for the first Apollo moon mission – 4GB compared to the 4K of *Apollo 11*.

* **The world's deepest gold mine is seven kilometres below the surface of the Earth.**

* Airports that are at higher altitudes require a longer airstrip due to lower air density.

* **Honolulu is the only place in the United States that has a royal palace.**

* The tallest known iceberg in the North Atlantic was 550 feet high.

* **More than 3,000 people work on research stations in Antarctica each year.**

* An atom bomb accidentally fell from a US plane over New Mexico in 1957. It left a sizeable crater but did not detonate.

* **One measly gallon of used motor oil can pollute approximately one million gallons of fresh water.**

```
A sperm can stay frozen
for 21 years before
being past its
use-by date.
```

* The *USS Abraham Lincoln* has five gyms on the ship and a basketball league with 22 teams.

* An Iranian man has been living in France's Charles de Gaulle airport since 1988.

Gandhi served twice with the British Army.

* The range of a medieval longbow is 220 yards.

* One in ten American soldiers is a Texan.

* Lebanon is the only country in the Middle East without a desert.

* Testing an F1 car in a wind tunnel costs £850 per hour.

* The Boeing 737 is nicknamed "Fat Albert".

* The Molotov cocktail was named after Vyacheslav Molotov, the Soviet minister of foreign affairs responsible for the 1939 invasion of Finland.

In July 1981, a tortoise was sentenced to death for murder in the eastern Kenyan village of Kyuasini.

* Cuba is the only island in the Caribbean to have a railway.

* **The most common name in Italy is Mario Rossi.**

* Goldfish are able to see in ultraviolet and infrared light.

* **Native Americans did not invent scalping. The practice was actually invented by the Scythians – a warlike people of southern Russia.**

* Pele is a nickname that the football legend earned while playing "pelada" – a rough version of the game played on the streets in Brazil.

* Even though Scotland gave the game of golf to the world, it was banned several times in the country in the 15th century as a military precaution.

* **George W Bush and John Kerry are 16th cousins three times removed.**

* The Schipol airport in Amsterdam has a special lounge that serves pre-flight meals to travelling cattle.

* **Play-Doh was actually developed as a wallpaper-cleaning solution.**

* Homing pigeons follow man-made roads to find their destinations.

The space between your eyebrows is called the glabella.

* **The first documented "cock rings" were made in the 13th century using goats' eyelashes.**

* Horatio Nelson's body was brought back to England in a barrel of brandy so it wouldn't decompose.

* The world land speed record for reversing is 102mph.

* Two British Prime Ministers, Lord Winchilsea and George Canning, have fought duels – one of them while still in office.

* Wild West souvenir hunters disconnected North America's first transcontinental railway as soon as it was built.

```
Sloths are
the world's
slowest mammals,
with a top speed
of 0.07 miles
per hour.
```

* Germany's national anthem was once sung to the same tune as *God Save The Queen*.

Nuts PUB AMMO

* The meaning of the word "maverick" comes from a Texas rancher, Samuel Maverick, who could never be bothered to brand his cattle.

The four ghosts that chase Pac-Man around his maze are called Inky, Blinky, Pinky and Clyde.

* **During World War I, no Allied pilot was equipped with a parachute.**

* *The Sopranos* was almost called Family Man because of fears that viewers might think the show was about opera.

* **Ireland is the largest consumer of canned baked beans in the world.**

* It is medically possible to keep a severed head alive.

* **The "Year Knife" holds the record for having the most blades: 2,000.**

> The longest-ever
> recorded flight
> of a chicken is
> 13 seconds.

* A human hair can support up to 100g and can stretch one-and-a-half times its own length before it snaps.

* **Most real ales are filtered through something called isinglass, which is a mixture made from fish bladders.**

* Domestic dogs and cats were the cause of 9,600 accidents to humans in 2003.

* **The *Voyager* spacecraft travels at 38,000mph.**

* *Jaws 2* was originally going to be called More Jaws, but test audiences thought the film was going to be a spoof.

* Pac-Man was originally called Puckman. It was changed to stop vandals turning the "P" in Puck into an "F" on the game cabinet.

* A 1,000-egg omelette is traditionally eaten on the Friday before Lent in Ponti, Italy.

* **The correct name for Bangkok is Krung Thep.**

* The most decorated US soldier of all time was Vietnam vet Joe Hooper. He earned 37 medals and was credited with killing 115 Vietcong.

* **Human bone is as strong as granite in supporting weight. A block the size of a matchbox can support nine tonnes.**

Banging your head against a wall will burn 150 calories an hour.

* The catacombs beneath Paris are said to contain at least three million corpses.

* The word "Tory" began life as an insult. It comes from the Irish word "toiridhe", used to describe Irish robbers.

There are more plastic flamingos in the US than real ones.

* The British Royal Family was renamed Windsor by a commoner (George V's private secretary) because of anti-German feeling during WWI.

* Animals are allowed to attend church services on St Anthony's Day in Mexico.

* The original name of the Bloody Tower in the Tower Of London was the Garden Tower.

* The Americans created the CIA based on a suggestion by the British in 1940.

* There's still an estimated 100,000 tonnes of gold left in the ground of California.

* Mexico City is slowly sinking at a rate of eight inches per year because it was built on top of an underground reservoir.

* *The Office* originally had a voiceover narration by John "Bergerac" Nettles but it was removed. Obviously...

* During a big speech, Hitler claimed to lose 5–6lb in sweat.

* Rats' teeth are as hard as steel and exert a biting pressure of 7,000 pounds per square inch.

```
We get goosebumps where our
cave-dwelling ancestors used
to have body hair.
```

* M Night Shyamalan, director of *The Village*, made up his middle name when he was a teenager.

* Rachel Stevens' feet are partially webbed.

> Jennifer Ellison was a world senior ballet champion at the age of 14.

✳ The only living creature known to have been killed by an extraterrestrial object was a dog – struck by a small meteorite in Egypt in 1911.

✳ If a pinhead was brought to the same temperature as the sun's core (15,000,000°C), it would set light to everything for 60 miles around.

✳ The motorbike used by Steve McQueen in *The Great Escape* is the same one used by The Fonz in *Happy Days*.

✳ In 1960, an American rocket crashed in Cuba, killing a cow. The cow was given an official funeral by the government as a victim of "imperialist aggression".

✳ The flag of Paraguay is the only national flag that is not the same on both sides.

* A slice of moon rock is sealed in the stained glass of Washington Cathedral in dedication to the Apollo astronauts.

* **The largest iceberg ever recorded in the southern Pacific Ocean was larger than Belgium.**

`A mature oak tree sheds 700,000 leaves every autumn.`

* Ancient Romans found guilty of murdering their fathers were put in a sack with a dog, a cock and a viper and then drowned.

* **The Earth increases in weight by around 25 tonnes every day. The extra tonnage is "space dust".**

* James Bond's sworn enemy SMERSH is a real KGB department, named after its motto "Smert Shpionen", meaning "Death to Spies".

* **Stopping from 200mph to 0mph, the Aston Martin Vantage 600's brakes produce enough energy to heat a one-bedroom flat for a fortnight.**

* Tony Hawk has been a professional skateboarder since he was 14 years old.

```
Bats always turn left
when leaving a cave.
```

* **Hawaii is the only US state that grows coffee commercially.**

* Downtown Athens boasts 200 legal brothels.

* **Surgeons who play video games cut down mistakes during operations by 37 per cent.**

* There is no Albanian word for "headache".

* **There are 49 germs per square inch on a toilet seat.**

* There is a museum in the USA dedicated solely to spoons – 5,400 of them.

* **9,350,000 diseases are sexually transmitted every day.**

* The USA and Russia are, at their closest point, only 2.5 miles apart.

* **The only 15-letter word that can be spelled without repeating a letter is "uncopyrightable".**

* Mazda cars are named after the Persian god of light.

* **French fries originated in Belgium.**

* Lumberjacks have the highest mortality rate of any worker: 117.8 deaths per 100,000.

The chances of dying during a game of five-a-side football are one in 25,000.

* **Only one person in two billion will live to be 116 or older.**

* Italy's national flag was designed by Napoleon Bonaparte.

Each day is longer than the one it follows by 0.00000002 seconds because the Earth's spin is gradually slowing down.

* **Sideburns were named after US Civil War general Ambrose Burnside, who sported a hefty pair of mutton chops in battle.**

* A beaver fells more than 200 trees in a single year.

* **In the time it takes a Nissan Micra 1.3 to reach 60mph, the Lamborghini Diablo GT can go from 0-100mph and back to 0mph.**

* The top air ace of World War I was Royal Air Force pilot Edward Mannock, with 73 kills.

* The first ready-to-eat breakfast cereal was Shredded Wheat in 1893, beating Kellogg's Corn Flakes by five years.

* A ten-stone person would weigh 7lb on Pluto.

* At any given time, there's an average of 61,000 people airborne over the USA.

* The average cost of rehabilitating each seal after the 1989 Exxon Valdez oil spill in Alaska was $80,000.

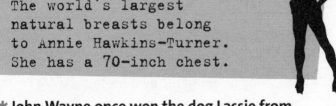

The world's largest natural breasts belong to Annie Hawkins-Turner. She has a 70-inch chest.

* John Wayne once won the dog Lassie from its owner in a poker game.

* Telly Savalas and Tommy Lee both had mothers who won the Miss Greece beauty contest.

> One billion people don't have
> clean drinking water.

* It takes 3,000 cows to supply America's NFL with a year's worth of footballs.

* Steven Spielberg directed the first episode of *Columbo*.

* The most common procedure conducted by US military surgeons during WWII – even at the height of the fighting – was circumcision.

* Charlie Chaplin's dead body was stolen and held to ransom.

* The odds of being hit by a meteorite are 200 million to one.

* Ten per cent of the Russian government's income comes from sales of vodka.

* Steven Seagal was the first non-Asian to open a martial arts academy in Japan.

* In the film *Pearl Harbor*, Kate Beckinsale is seen wearing a bikini – even though the bikini wasn't invented until 1946 (five years after the attack).

* **The most impossible item to flush down a toilet is a ping-pong ball.**

* Michael Schumacher got his big break in motorsport when he replaced Jordan's Bertrand Gachot, who was jailed for spraying CS gas in a London cabbie's face in 1991.

* **At any given moment, there are some 1,800 thunderstorms around the world.**

A fighter pilot wears more layers of clothing than a medieval knight would have.

* There are, on average, 6,000 computer viruses released every month.

* In most of continental Europe, wedding rings are worn on the right hand.

* Cats can make over 100 vocal sounds; dogs only ten.

* The average adult falls asleep seven minutes after their head hits the pillow.

* It would take 288 years to spend a night in every hotel room in Las Vegas.

A boomerang is effective at killing game up to 150m away.

* Peter Kay's school metalwork teacher was Steve Coogan's dad.

* Pope John Paul II was an honorary Harlem Globetrotter.

* Pain travels through our bodies at a speed of 350 feet per second.

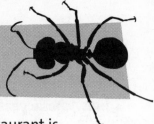

An ant can survive
for two weeks
underwater.

✱ In Iceland, tipping in a restaurant is
considered an insult.

✱ **Forest fires move faster uphill than downhill.**

✱ The expression "rule of thumb" derives
from an old English law, which stated that
you couldn't beat your wife with anything
wider than your thumb.

✱ **The end opposite the striking face on a
hammer is called a peen.**

✱ Bombay duck hasn't got anything to do
with duck – it's dried fish.

✱ **There is no word in the English language
that rhymes with orange, silver, purple
or month.**

* Grapes explode when put in a microwave.

* **The average American eats almost 200 sandwiches a year.**

* Six out of seven gynaecologists are men.

* **The lime that's served in the top of a bottle of Corona is not supposed to go into the beer. Its use in Mexico is purely as a stopper to keep flies out.**

* Spiral staircases in Britain's medieval castles ran clockwise so that attacking knights couldn't use their right hand – the sword hand – while descending knights could.

* **The armadillo is the only other animal besides humans that can catch leprosy.**

Charles Manson unsuccessfully auditioned for The Monkees.

* Pirates wore earrings in the belief that it would improve their eyesight.

A violin contains about 70 separate pieces of wood.

* **It's possible to tell a man's fingerprints from a woman's.**

* The twelfth most spoken language in the world is Javanese.

* **Forty-three million McDonald's burgers are eaten throughout the world every day.**

* The chance of being on a plane that is hijacked by terrorists twice in the same year is one in 150 million.

* **The waxworks of Eric Cantona, Frank Bruno, Shane Warne, John Major and Robert Carlyle were removed from Madame Tussaud's last year.**

A group of geese on the ground is a gaggle; a group of geese in the air is a skein.

* The first Englishman to be killed in an aviation accident was Mr Rolls of Rolls-Royce fame.

* **Sir Winston Churchill smoked an estimated 300,000 cigars in his lifetime.**

* The Mona Lisa has no eyebrows. It was the fashion in Renaissance Florence to shave them off.

* **Mexican president Antonio de Santa Anna held a funeral for his own amputated leg.**

* Oliver Cromwell banned kissing on Sundays on pain of a prison sentence.

* **Vic Reeves bought Tom Baker's house near Maidstone in Kent.**

* In 400BC, the Greek city of Sparta was made up of 25,000 citizens and 500,000 slaves.

* **The world's oldest piece of toilet paper is thought to be 1,200 years old.**

* The first person in Britain to own a videophone was Jeremy Beadle.

* **The average number of patients per doctor in the UK is 2,000.**

* An adult sleeping with another adult in a standard bed has less personal space than a baby in a cot.

* **Handling, processing and storing cash costs Britain's banks and businesses £4bn a year.**

A male rat can impregnate 20 females in six hours.

* Michelangelo's cook was illiterate, so he drew her a shopping list, which is now priceless.

✳ **A bee is more likely to sting you on a windy day.**

Every year there are only around a dozen fatal shark attacks. In return, we kill 100 million sharks every year.

✳ There are 296 steps to the top of the Leaning Tower of Pisa.

✳ **Pollen lasts forever.**

✳ If 20-a-day smokers inhaled a week's worth of nicotine, they would die instantly.

✳ **If a telephone directory was brought within six metres of the gravitational pull of a black hole, it would weigh a million million tonnes.**

✳ The average prison sentence in the US is 28 months.

* **Between 100 and 200 people die each year because of deer running in front of cars.**

* Britain's first National Lottery was in 1567, to pay for public works. There were 400,000 tickets sold at ten shillings each.

* **Obese truck drivers have twice as many traffic accidents as healthy ones.**

* Puerto Rico's Arecibo telescope, the largest in the world, is the size of ten billion bowls of cornflakes.

* **Martial arts hero Jet Li turned down roles in both *Matrix* sequels.**

* The year 46BC went on for 445 days, while Julius Caesar restructured the Julian calendar.

Charlie Chaplin once came
third in a Charlie Chaplin
lookalike contest.

* **Rachel Weisz's father invented the artificial respirator.**

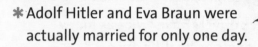

```
Roosters can't crow
if their necks are
fully extended.
```

* Adolf Hitler and Eva Braun were actually married for only one day.

* **In 1971, Germany became the first European country to have a McDonald's.**

* British GPs prescribe an average of 6.3 items per person per year.

* **Al Capone's business cards claimed he was a used-furniture salesman.**

* There's an Icelandic multiplex cinema with six screens but only 17 seats.

* **The motto of Honolulu's police force is, "Serving and protecting with Aloha".**

* Bob Marley's father was white and came from Liverpool.

* **The "bracing" smell at the seaside is usually caused by rotting seaweed.**

* The average career span for a "seeing eye" dog is seven to ten years.

* **Los Angeles has one of the worst highway bottlenecks in the world – it causes 27,144,000 hours of gridlock each year.**

* The air around a meteor is up to 60,000°K (Kelvin) – ten times the surface temperature of the sun.

* **Bill Paxton is the only actor to have played characters killed by a Terminator, a Predator and an Alien.**

Naturalists use marshmallows to lure alligators out of swamps.

* The Rock has a degree in criminology and planned to become a secret service agent.

* **Bill Clinton was paid the largest ever advance for a non-fiction book: $10million.**

All the clocks in the film *Pulp Fiction* are stuck on 4.20.

* A pint of hot water is lighter than a pint of cold water because it is less dense.

* **White berries are almost always poisonous.**

* The first victim of the Allied bombing of Berlin in WWII was the city zoo's only elephant.

* **The US spent $21bn dollars on prison construction and maintenance last year.**

* The most popular cosmetic surgery procedure among men is liposuction.

* Ninety per cent of all writing uses the same 1,000 words.

* Actor James Woods filed a report with an airline after flying with four suspicious men who turned out to be 9/11 hijackers.

* According to the book *Love For Sale*, three in four men pay for sex while visiting Asia or Africa.

* In the womb of the sand tiger shark, the first embryo to hatch eats the remaining eggs for nutrition.

* The face of a penny can hold 30 droplets of water.

* The deepest lake in the world is Lake Baikal in Russia.

A pigeon can't lay an egg unless she sees another pigeon.

* Hitler was voted *Time* magazine's "Man Of The Year" in 1938.

* In the US, quad bikes accounted for 84,900 injuries in just one year.

Coprastasophobia is the fear of constipation.

* In 2003 there were 422 reported kidnappings in Mexico City.

* Black Eyed Peas sexpot Fergie started out on the Disney Channel's *Kids Incorporated*.

* During eight hours of sleep, most people spend two hours dreaming, split into four periods of 30 minutes.

* It takes eight hours to drive across the state of Nebraska.

* Every human is naturally radioactive.

* There's a one in 2.8 million chance that you'll die by falling down a hole.

* **The largest volcano in the solar system is called Olympus Mons and is found on our near-neighbour, Mars. It is nearly three times higher than Everest.**

* The first living creatures ever to be transported by air were a sheep, a rooster and a duck.

```
The great pyramids of Egypt now
stand a full three miles
south of the spot where
they were originally
built because of the
shifting of the earth.
```

* **The longest siege in history lasted 29 years when the Egyptians besieged Azotus (now Asdod) in Israel.**

* Joshua Slocum, the first man to sail solo around the world, couldn't swim.

* **The Amazonian Nambiquara tribe has no numerical system.**

* Pollen from pine trees is able to travel far enough for a Scottish pine to be pollinated by a Norwegian one.

Peanuts are one of the ingredients of dynamite.

* **Up until the 18th century, British sailors were allowed a daily ration of one pint of neat rum.**

* A three-wheeled vehicle powered by dogs was scrapped in 1880 after an outcry by animal lovers.

* *Psycho* **was the first Hollywood film to show a toilet flushing.**

* In 1986, Nathan Hicks of St Louis, Missouri, shot his brother, Herbert, dead because he used six toilet rolls in two days.

* The brain weighs only three pounds but uses 20 per cent of the body's blood and oxygen.

* Strawberries have more vitamin C than oranges.

* The average lifespan of a parrot is 120 years.

* There is one square mile to every resident of Alaska.

* Lachanophobia is the fear of vegetables.

Celery has negative calories - it takes more energy to chew up and digest the vegetable than it actually contains.

* Over 300 dogs a year are registered for US military service.

* The average British marriage lasts nine years and ten months.

* Sheffield has the most public lavatories in Britain.

* Jamie Lynn-Sigler, who plays Meadow in *The Sopranos*, couldn't be less Italian. She's actually part Cuban, Greek, Romanian and Sephardic Jew.

* Four out of five French chickens are free range. In Britain, it's one in 50.

Russian men have an average life expectancy of 57.

* Investment bank Goldman Sachs employs nearly 700 "managing directors".

* Approximately 50 Bibles are sold around the world every minute.

* In Tokyo, a bicycle is faster than a car for most trips of less than 50 minutes.

* Hummingbirds can't walk.

* The king of hearts is the only king without a moustache on a standard playing card.

* Your body creates and kills 15 million red blood cells per second.

* Until the 19th century, solid blocks of tea were used as money in Siberia.

* Halle Berry is named after a department store in Ohio where she grew up.

* A Boeing 747 holds 57,285 gallons of fuel.

* It takes glass one million years to decompose.

Bananas are actually considered to be the world's largest herb because they contain no wood fibre.

* Over 2,500 left-handed people a year are killed from using products made for right-handed people.

* Pinocchio is Italian for "pine eye".

* **Every 45 seconds, a house catches fire in the United States.**

* Of all the words in the English language, the word "set" has the most definitions.

```
The human body contains enough
iron to make a peg that would
be strong enough to hang a
human body on.
```

* **Heidi Klum's left leg is insured for more (£1.2million) than her right leg (£1million) because the right has a scar on it that she picked up from rollerblading.**

* The world's largest body of fresh water, Lake Superior in North America, contains 2,935 cubic miles of water.

* **The giant sloth sleeps for 17 hours a day, yet dreams for just 70 minutes.**

* Dannii Minogue appeared in an advert for Penguin biscuits.

* **Today's average household contains more computer power than existed in the entire world before 1965.**

* EU bureaucrats get through 1.5 billion sheets of paper a year. That's 15 tonnes every day.

* **Toilet paper was first made in 1880 by the British Perforated Paper Co.**

The world's largest toad was the same size as the world's smallest antelope.

* UK shoppers use eight billion plastic bags a year.

* **In 1996, vandals wrecked a bunker in Austria that was designed to withstand an atomic bomb.**

* Your bed is home to two million mites.

* If all the living creatures on Earth were weighed together, ants would make up 15 per cent of the total weight.

If your body's natural defences failed, the bacteria in your stomach would consume you within 48 hours.

* A third of CDs on sale are thought to be pirate copies.

* In the 17th century, Queen Christine of Sweden had a four-inch cannon built so she could fire miniature cannonballs at the fleas in her room.

* 24's Elisha Cuthbert used to host a show called *Popular Mechanics For Kids*.

* The largest private company in the world is the Indian railway system, which employs around 1.6 million people.

* There were 15,000 TV sets in Britain in 1946. There are now over 55 million.

* **Donald Duck comics were banned in Finland because he doesn't wear pants.**

* Humans can catch 65 different diseases from dogs.

```
During World War II,
it was against
the law in Germany
to name a horse Adolf.
```

* **The 358 richest people in the world own as much as the poorest three billion.**

* Mongolia's Ulan Bator is the coldest capital city in the world.

* **In the 18th century, the London Stock Exchange had its own brothel.**

* The speed of the Earth depends on where you are, from 1,600km/h at the equator to zero at the poles. In London, it is 998km/h.

Hot water freezes quicker than cold water does.

* **Protons are so small there are 500,000,000,000 of them on the dot of an "i".**

* A metal coat hanger is 44 inches long when straightened.

* **The Catholic Church is the largest landowner in New York City.**

* Two-thirds of all urban space is used for transportation.

* **Dalmatians and humans are the only mammals with the same kind of urine.**

* Most elephants weigh less than a blue whale's tongue.

The Exorcist is the highest grossing horror movie of all time.

Native speakers of Japanese learn Spanish much more easily than they learn English.

The thief who drives your car away is 200 times more likely to crash it than you are.

At the time of Shakespeare, everyone had roughly 16,000 ancestors alive.

Paris Hilton is so popular in Japan that she travels in disguise.

Thomas Edison, the inventor of the light bulb, was afraid of the dark.

A scientist discovered phosphorus while he was trying to turn urine into gold.

Croatia was the first country to recognise the United States of America, in 1776.

* Mobile ringtones account for ten per cent of the music industry's global revenue.

* **James Dean was given a speeding ticket just two hours before the car crash that killed him.**

* The US has more bagpipe bands than Scotland.

* **Elvis Presley never gave an encore.**

* The arch at the new Wembley Stadium is visible up to 28 miles away.

* **Trivia was the Roman goddess of crossroads. The word "trivia" is derived from the spot in ancient Rome where three roads linked and women met to exchange gossip, which was, therefore, the talk of the Tri (three) Via (roads).**

In the span of a lifetime, an average man is likely to shave 20,000 times.

* When splattered blood droplets are shaped like bowling pins, it usually means a struggle took place.

* **The loudest ever human scream was 129 decibels. To give some context, a chainsaw registers 120 decibels while in use.**

* A newborn kangaroo would fit in a teaspoon.

Polar bears can eat 150lb of meat in one sitting.

* **As long as no excessive water is lost through sweat, the body can survive up to 14 days without water.**

* The drinking straw was invented in 1886 by Josephine Cochran.

* **The heaviest snowfall in 24 hours was 192.5cm – recorded at Silver Lake, Colorado, on 14/15 April 1921.**

* Mornings last for a week on the moon.

* **The Caspian Sea is, in fact, the world's largest lake.**

* Juliet actually stands on the floor beside the upper window during the famous "balcony" scene in *Romeo and Juliet*.

* **To find out the approximate number of hours a corpse has been dead, you need to subtract the rectal temperature from 98.6°F and divide by 1.5.**

* When offered a new pen to try out, a whopping 97 per cent of people will write their own name.

South American gauchos put raw steak under their saddles at the start of a day's riding to tenderise the meat.

* **Until the 18th century, India produced almost all of the world's diamonds.**

 Nuts PUB AMMO

* Half the world's population has seen at least one James Bond movie.

* *The Empire Strikes Back* is the lowest-grossing of all *Star Wars* films.

* Your tongue is the only muscle in your body that is attached at just one end.

* A Rubik's Cube has 1,929,770,126,028,800 different colour combinations.

Sylvester Stallone used to clean out lion cages for a living.

* It's illegal to use a lasso to catch a fish in Tennessee.

* Nintendo was established in 1889 and started out making playing cards.

* According to official FBI stats, bank robberies are least likely to occur on Tuesday mornings.

* During the first Gulf War, the *USS Acadia* destroyer was nicknamed "The Love Boat" because ten per cent of the women aboard became pregnant while deployed.

* Non-smokers dream more than smokers.

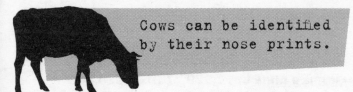

Cows can be identified by their nose prints.

* NASA estimates that a space shuttle faces a one-in-250 chance of colliding with space junk.

* A lion's and a tiger's roar, combined and run backwards, were used to make King Kong's roar for the original movie.

* A tonne of Mexican marijuana fetches $1.6billion wholesale in the US.

* The world record for stone skipping over water is 38 skips.

Nuts PUB AMMO

* **Cheerleading accounts for 54 per cent of all injuries among female athletes in US high schools and colleges.**

* Fonzie's leather jacket is on display at the American History Smithsonian in Washington, D.C.

* **The weight of a standard-issue loaded M16 is 8.8lb.**

* The Utah Jazz NBA team has custom-made eight-foot-long beds in its rooms at Las Vegas' Palms Casino.

The average nipple size is 0.27 inches for women and 0.22 inches for men.

* **Ohio State Reformatory, Ohio, served as the set for *The Shawshank Redemption*.**

* Dr Seuss invented the word "nerd" in his book *If I Ran The Zoo*.

＊ **Only female mosquitoes bite.**

＊ The word "lethologica" means not being able to remember the particular word you want.

＊ **Bamboo can grow as fast as three whole feet in just one day.**

＊ The longest one-syllable word in the English language is "screeched".

The side of a hammer is called a cheek.

＊ **A chameleon's tongue is twice as long as its body.**

＊ Himalaya literally means "home of snow".

＊ **Just one in 50 self-described "authors" is ever published.**

＊ Over 20 million Mexican free-tail bats live in Bracken Cave, Texas.

* **A rhinoceros' horn is made of compacted hair.**

* A female silkworm gives off sexual pheromones at four-billionths of an ounce per second – enough to excite every male silkworm within a mile.

* **The Golden Gate Bridge connects two different areas that, at one time, were 1,000 miles apart.**

* The Sanskrit word for war translates as "wanting more cows".

* **By flying in a "V" formation, birds nearly double the distance they are able to fly.**

* A human being's teeth are five per cent water.

```
The fastest-moving muscle in
your body is the one that opens
and closes the eyelid.
```

* **Tigers have striped skin, not just striped fur.**

* There are 336 dimples on a regulation golf ball.

The pupils in goats' and sheep's eyes are rectangular.

* **For every four climbers who make it to the summit of Mount Everest, one will die in the attempt.**

* Ninety per cent of American homes have a tub of ice cream in the freezer.

* **American airports found $250,436.65 in change between October 2003 and July 2004, all of which was claimed by the US government.**

* If you sail due west or due east from Cape Horn, on the southern tip of Chile, the next landmass you'll hit is Cape Horn again.

* **More people die playing golf than any other sport.**

* Sexy supermodel Victoria Silvstedt is a former Miss Sweden.

* **The sound made by the Victoria Falls in Zimbabwe can be heard 40 miles away.**

* The top health-related internet search for men between 18 and 35 is "pregnancy".

* **A straw holds one-and-a-half teaspoons of water.**

* The first home microwave cost £988.

```
142 men in Britain are
injured every year by
the holding pins found
in new shirts.
```

* **A human eyeball weighs 1oz.**

* Less than one per cent of the Caribbean islands are inhabited.

* A metal sphere the size of a tennis ball travelling in space is as lethal as 25 sticks of dynamite if it hits anything.

* Forty-eight per cent of UK internet users say they couldn't manage without the web for two weeks.

```
A bowling pin has to tilt
7.5 degrees to fall down.
```

* The lifespan of an eyelash is about five months.

* The volume of water moving in any one of the Earth's "big five" ocean currents is 50 times that of the world's rivers combined.

* Mexico once had three presidents in a single day.

* *The Simple Life* star Nicole Richie doesn't know who her biological father is. Lionel Richie is her adopted dad.

* The Pentagon has twice as many toilets as necessary. When it was built, Virginia still had segregation laws requiring separate toilets for blacks and whites.

* Grapes are grown more frequently than any other fruit worldwide.

* The University of Alaska covers four time zones.

* One glass of milk can give a person a .02 blood-alcohol concentration on a breathalyser test.

* The biggest ever cheese was 6ft high and 32ft long. Made in Quebec, Canada, the 57,508lb cheddar was equivalent to the amount of cheese eaten by 2,500 Canadians in a year.

During the Middle Ages, people used spider webs to try to cure warts.

* According to statistics, silver cars are half as likely to crash as white cars.

* **The shape of the *Millennium Falcon* from *Star Wars* was inspired by a hamburger with a bite taken from it.**

There are 5,800 Academy Award voters who decide on Oscar nominations.

* Winston Churchill was granted honorary US citizenship by Congress in 1963.

* **Napoleon made his battle plans in a sandpit.**

* The first sport to have a world championships was billiards in 1873.

* **Ants stretch when they wake up in the morning.**

* Alcohol is considered proper payment for teachers among the Lepcha people of Tibet.

* A ticket to travel on Virgin's *VSS Enterprise* three-hour, zero-gravity flight, which begins in 2007, will cost £100,000.

* Americans eat approximately 20 billion pickles every year.

* A "G" is the force of the Earth's gravity. You pull one "G" just sitting on the sofa watching football.

We use 54 muscles every time we take a step forward.

* Global warming is raising the temperature of your testicles.

* Only 20 per cent of Americans have passports.

* A woodchuck breathes only ten times during hibernation.

* Between the ages of 20 and 70, the average man will have 700 hours of sex.

* On New Year's Day in 1907, Theodore Roosevelt shook hands with no less than 8,150 people at the White House.

* **Only 13.5 per cent of scientists are women.**

* Carnivorous animals will not eat another animal that has been hit by lightning.

Screwdrivers were first invented to help knights put on armour.

* **More than 10,000 birds a year die from smashing into windows.**

* Forty-nine different kinds of food are mentioned in the Bible.

* **Sir Isaac Newton was an ordained minister in the Church of England.**

* The number one source of employment in Afghanistan is mine clearance.

* **British MPs are not allowed to mention the House of Lords. Instead, they call it "the other place".**

* McDonald's feeds over 46 million people a day, which is more than the entire population of Spain.

```
The largest cell in the human
body is the ovum - the smallest
is the sperm.
```

* **The sport with the highest ratio of officials to participants is tennis.**

* The drugs required to execute a death-row criminal cost $86.06.

* **Twenty-two per cent of the British public visit a fish and chip shop at least once a week.**

* Every year, we leave 105 million answerphone messages.

* Britons eat, on average, 2.2 curries a week – spending £1.5billion in total every single year.

* A scientific satellite only needs 250 watts of power to operate.

There are 934 million people on the internet worldwide.

* Abraham Lincoln's mother died when the family dairy cow ate poisonous mushrooms and Mrs Lincoln drank the milk.

* Pepper was sold in individual grains during Elizabethan times.

* A single bale of cotton can make up to 215 pairs of jeans.

* During each second of the 90-second lift-off, a space shuttle's engines consume enough fuel to power two million cars.

* **Nanotechnology has produced a guitar no bigger than a blood cell – ten micrometres long.**

* X-ray technology has shown that there are three different versions of the Mona Lisa underneath the one that's visible.

* **The pressure in a bottle of champagne is about 90lb per square inch. That's about three times the pressure of a car tyre.**

The corkscrew was invented in 1860.

* To see a rainbow, you must have your back to the sun.

* **Minus 40°C is exactly the same temperature as 40°F.**

* Seven per cent of the entire Irish barley crop goes into the making of Guinness.

* To help aid digestion, crocodiles keep rocks – up to 15lb in weight – stored in their stomachs.

The people of East Anglia used to mummify cats and place them in the walls of their homes to ward off evil spirits.

* Dannii Minogue has twice been bitten by poisonous spiders.

* U2 used to be a five-piece band until The Edge's brother left to form The Virgin Prunes.

* Australia's ex-prime minister Bob Hawke once held the world record time for beer drinking – managing to down 2.5 pints in just 12 seconds.

* A man burns 87 calories taking off a woman's bra with his teeth.

* The script used for *Ocean's Twelve* was originally meant to be a John Woo film.

* **Around 29 million gallons of petroleum are spilled annually in North American oceans.**

* Of the computer viruses spread in the first six months of 2004, 70 per cent were created by 18-year-old German Sven Jaschan.

* **A ripe cranberry will bounce.**

* The first olive-powered power plant in Spain will be able to power 130,000 homes.

The people of China use a total of 45 billion chopsticks every year.

* **The *Jahre Viking* tanker is the largest ship in the world — it is 77 metres longer than the Empire State Building is tall.**

* Christopher Lee has been in almost 300 movies and TV productions.

* **Soda water does not contain soda.**

> The average cow produces 90 glasses of milk a day.

* During "hell week" training, US Navy SEALs get just four hours of sleep in five-and-a-half days.

* **The largest toy distributor in the world is McDonald's.**

* The largest cork tree in the world is in Portugal. It averages more than one tonne of raw cork per harvest. That's enough to cork 100,000 bottles.

* **Catherine Zeta-Jones broke into show business as a teenaged Shirley Bassey impersonator.**

* After the Sioux defeated Custer at Little Bighorn, tribal chief Sitting Bull became an entertainer and toured America with Buffalo Bill's Wild West show.

* **Humphrey Bogart was related to Princess Diana. They were seventh cousins.**

* Genghis Khan's cavalry rode female horses so that soldiers could drink their milk.

* **Woodpecker scalps, porpoise teeth and giraffe tails have all been used as money.**

A cat lover is called an ailurophile, while a cat hater is an ailurophobe.

* If China imported just ten per cent of its rice needs, the world price would increase by 80 per cent.

* **An inch of snow falling evenly on one acre of ground is equivalent to about 2,715 gallons of water.**

* The oldest ever base jumper is 74 years old.

* There are 240 white dots in a Pac-Man arcade game.

* Eau de cologne was originally marketed as a way of protecting yourself against the plague.

* Cuckoo clocks come from Germany's Black Forest – not Switzerland.

The "you are here" arrow on a map is called the "IDEO locator".

* The warrior tribes of Ethiopia used to tie the testicles of those they killed in battle to the ends of their spears.

* In Zambia, tourists can't take pictures of Pygmies.

* Monopoly was originally rejected by its manufacturer for having 52 fundamental errors.

* In the Andes, time is often measured by how long it takes to smoke a cigarette.

* There are two credit cards for every person in the United States.

If you took one pound of cobwebs and spread them out in a straight line, it would go twice around the Earth.

* A fully-loaded supertanker travelling at normal speed takes at least 20 minutes to stop.

* Jenna Jameson's book *How To... Make Love Like A Porn Star* has sold so well that it has already had to be reprinted seven times.

* The first CIA officer charged with espionage was paid £49,000 by the KGB for information.

* The English Channel is two feet higher on the French side, due to centrifugal force.

* **The earliest recorded naval battle in British waters was in AD 719.**

* Clouds fly higher during the day than at night.

A car travelling at 100mph would reach the sun in just over 106 years.

* **Virginia extends farther west than West Virginia.**

* The US government spent £147,500 on "pickle research" in 1993.

* **Salt is the only rock that humans can eat.**

* Four men were executed for Abraham Lincoln's assassination.

* **There are 22 stars surrounding the mountain on the Paramount Pictures logo.**

* A woman called Carolyn Shoemaker has discovered 32 comets and approximately 300 asteroids.

* **The three best-known Western names in China are: Jesus Christ, Richard Nixon and Elvis Presley.**

Aztec emperor Montezuma had a nephew, Cuitlahac, whose name meant "plenty of excrement".

* The literal translation of kung fu is "leisure time".

* **There will be 107 incorrect medical procedures performed by the end of the day today.**

* In Spanish, the word Colgate translates into the command "Go hang yourself".

* **Superman's name on Krypton was Kal-El.**

Nuts PUB AMMO

* Fourteen million people perished in World War I, but 20 million died in the following flu epidemic.

* **One in four homeless South Koreans has a credit card.**

* The final hotdog sold at the Montreal Expos' last home baseball game was auctioned off for $2,161.

Taxi is spelled the same way in English, French, German, Swedish, Spanish, Danish, Norwegian, Dutch, Czech and Portuguese.

* **Reggie Strickland is the worst boxer in history. He has a record of 65 wins and 268 losses.**

* Robert De Niro was so pale as a child that kids called him "Bobby Milk".

* **The pocket gopher can run backwards as fast as it can run forwards.**

* McDonald's in Sweden sold a "McAfrika" sandwich.

Evidently snubbing the Samaritans, squids sometimes commit suicide by eating their own tentacles.

* **English soldiers of the Hundred Years War were known by the French as "Les Goddamns" due to their propensity to swear.**

* Dom Joly was born in Lebanon.

* **Most people have lost 50 per cent of their taste buds by the time they reach the age of 60.**

* Citizens of Chile, Austria and Egypt can be imprisoned for not voting.

* **Armadillos can be house-trained.**

* There is a Burt Reynolds museum in Florida.

* **At the end of his life, Elvis' calorific intake was that of a baby elephant's.**

> The liquid inside young coconuts can be used as a substitute for blood plasma.

* Disneyland refused to let in men with long hair during the '70s.

* **The only bone to have never been broken in a skiing accident is one located in the inner ear.**

* Sophie Anderton lost her virginity a week before her 16th birthday.

* **Weightlifting is the national sport of Bulgaria.**

* South Africa has no fewer than 11 official languages.

* **A leech has 32 brains.**

* The quartz crystal in a wristwatch vibrates 32,768 times per second.

* **To this very day, Yeomen dressed in Tudor uniform search the cellars of the House of Commons for gunpowder.**

* There are more handwritten letters in existence by George Washington than there are by John F Kennedy.

* **The shortest intercontinental commercial flight is 17 miles, from Gibraltar (Europe) to Tangier (Africa).**

* Huge wine jugs were often used by the ancient Greeks as coffins.

In the 1500s, one in every 25 coffins was found to have scratch marks on the inside.

* **The word "Sunday" does not appear in the Bible.**

* Albert Einstein's last words will forever be lost, as the only person who was with him – a nurse – didn't speak German.

* **The most abundant metal in the Earth's crust is aluminium.**

* The most popular name for a pet in the United States is "Max".

A female ferret may die if she goes into heat and is unable to find a mate.

* **Genghis Khan started out life as a goat-herder.**

* Camel-hair brushes are not actually made from camel hair, but squirrel hair.

* **The most overdue book in the world was borrowed from Sidney Sussex College, Cambridge. It was returned 288 years later.**

* Strawberries are a member of the rose family.

* **Approximately .002 per cent of men can fellate themselves.**

* Fluorescent clothing was invented to prevent WWII soldiers falling victim to friendly fire.

* **Austria was the first country to use postcards.**

```
Some species of vulture can fly
as high as 30,000 feet.
```

* The opposite of "cross-eyed" is "wall-eyed".

* **Of a total of about 7,000 staff at Auschwitz, only 750 were ever brought to justice.**

* There are over 100 million light-sensitive cells in the retina.

* **Over 100,000 Brits quit the city for the country every year.**

* Sugar was added to chewing gum by a dentist.

* **Polar explorers will only move 500 yards a day.**

* Donald Duck's middle name is Fauntleroy.

* **Every time Beethoven sat down to write music, he poured ice water over his head.**

* The only character to have appeared in every Bond film, other than 007 himself, is Miss Moneypenny.

* **A dead body goes stiff within six to 12 hours of death.**

* It takes 40 minutes to hard-boil an ostrich egg.

* **Europe is the only continent without a desert.**

```
Everything weighs one per cent
less at the equator.
```

* Portland, Oregon, was named in a coin-toss in 1844. Heads was Portland, tails was Boston.

* **Our hearing is less sharp after eating too much.**

* Earth is the only planet in our solar system not named after a god.

* **India has more post offices than any other country in the world.**

Only after you lose half your hair in one given area can people tell if you're going bald.

* A vulture will never attack prey that is moving.

* **The first mosque in the US was built in 1893.**

* It takes about 150 days for a fingernail to grow from the cuticle to the tip.

* The Nurburgring racetrack in Germany is 13 miles long, has 147 corners and has claimed more than 200 lives.

* Amber was once thought to be solidified sunshine or the petrified tears of gods.

* Cleopatra used pomegranate seeds to make lipstick.

* The decibel was named after Alexander Graham Bell.

* "Honcho" comes from a Japanese word meaning "squad leader".

* Castro was voted Cuba's best schoolboy athlete in 1944.

* *NYPD Blue*'s Dennis Franz was in an elite airborne division in Vietnam.

```
Hamsters blink one eye at
a time.
```

* Kiwis lay the largest eggs (relative to body size) of any bird.

* **The word "sex" was coined in 1382.**

* Numbering houses in London's streets began only in 1764.

```
Montana mountain
goats sometimes butt so
hard that their hooves
fall off.
```

* **Clark Gable was listed on his birth certificate as a girl.**

* Mel Gibson broke his school record for the most beatings in a week (27).

* **Leonardo da Vinci invented an alarm clock that woke the sleeper by rubbing his feet.**

* A hedgehog's heart beats 190 times a minute but drops to 20 beats per minute during hibernation.

* **For this year's Super Bowl, 1.4million Americans bought new TVs.**

* Fashion oddball Karl Lagerfeld owns 40 iPods.

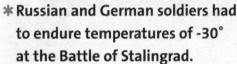

The only food cockroaches won't eat is cucumbers.

* **Russian and German soldiers had to endure temperatures of -30° at the Battle of Stalingrad.**

* Before mercury, brandy was used in thermometers.

* **Winston Churchill had a 90-gun salute at his state funeral.**

* When *Desperate Housewives'* Teri Hatcher posed nude, wrapped in nothing but Superman's cape, it became the most downloaded picture in internet history.

* The tug of war was an Olympic sport between 1900 and 1920.

* Scientists have observed some 450 animal species in gay relationships, including sheep, salmon and badgers.

* Eating poppy seeds can give a positive drug test.

* The human body contains enough lime to whitewash a small shed.

* A sloth can move twice as fast in water as it can on land.

In 1996, edible chip bags were introduced in Ireland for a trial period.

* Nauru is the only country in the world with no official capital.

* Napoleon had an enema every day.

Any space vehicle must move at a rate of seven miles per second in order to escape the Earth's gravitational pull.

* White wine gets darker as it ages, while red wine gets lighter.

* **During World War II, a group of alpine soldiers, stranded in mountain snows, survived for an entire month on nothing but a cask of sherry.**

* Horses, rabbits and rats can't vomit.

* **The Wembley Arch is 133m at its highest point – over four times the height of the original Twin Towers.**

* Steven Spielberg has only got one kidney.

* **The Queen is only 5ft 4ins tall.**

* For every "normal" web page, there are five porn pages.

* **Syphilis was known as the "French disease" in Italy and the "English disease" in France.**

The fight scene in Rocky was filmed in reverse, starting with round 15 and working back to round one, with the make-up removed after each round.

* A Slinky can stretch to 87ft.

* **Women buy four out of every ten condoms sold.**

* Tasmania has the cleanest air in the inhabited world.

* **Ethelred the Unready, King of England in the tenth century, spent his wedding night in bed with his wife and his mother-in-law.**

* The first recorded hole-in-one was in 1868.

* **Between the two World Wars, 40 different governments were in power in France.**

* Instant coffee has been around since the 18th century.

* **The Incas and Aztecs were able to function without the wheel.**

Curiously, a can of Spam is opened every four seconds.

* Homer Simpson's email address from *The Dad Who Knew Too Little* episode is Chunkylover53@aol.com.

* **Saint John was the only one of the 12 Apostles to die a natural death.**

* There are ten million bacteria in a pint of milk — that's the same number as the population of Greece.

* **Until 1898, Pepsi was known as "Brad's drink".**

Nuts PUB AMMO

* The Atlantic Ocean is about nine times the size of the USA.

* **Sir Bobby Charlton, Sir Tom Finney and Nat Lofthouse were all pallbearers for Sir Stanley Matthews.**

* Only four per cent of Brits are vegetarians.

The oldest captive goldfish on record lived for 43 years, in Yorkshire.

* **Mao Tse-Tung never brushed his teeth but washed his mouth with tea instead.**

* The lance ceased to be an official battle weapon in the British Army in 1927.

* **Bugs Bunny was originally called "Happy Rabbit".**

* The average Brit is 38 years old.

* The religion of the Todas people of southern India forbids them to cross any kind of bridge.

* American civil servants' payslips are recycled to make toilet rolls.

* The Bay of Fundy in Canada has the world's highest tides, rising and falling 53ft – the height of a three-storey building.

* Playing music containing augmented fourth chords used to be avoided because it was thought to invoke the Devil.

* The number of possible ways of playing the first four moves per side in a game of chess is 318,979,564,000.

The house fly only lives for 14 days.

* An elephant's trunk has 40,000 muscles but no bone.

* The first submarine was successfully launched in 1620.

* There is no single word for the back of the knee.

The longest recorded tapeworm found inside the human body was an astounding – and somewhat sickening – 33 metres.

* The entire collection of *The Encyclopaedia Britannica* weighs nine stone.

* A rat can last longer without water than a camel.

* A day on Mercury (sunrise to sunrise) is equivalent to 176 Earth days.

* In 1939, a five-year-old Peruvian girl gave birth to a baby boy.

* There are 602 rooms in Buckingham Palace.

* The average driver will be locked out of their car nine times during their lifetime.

* **There are four cars on the back of a US $10 bill.**

* On average, 700 grapes go into producing one bottle of wine.

* **A typist's left hand does 56 per cent of the work.**

The first toy product ever advertised on television was Mr Potato Head.

* The US is the only country with nuclear bombs on foreign soil – 480 spread out over Europe.

* **Walt Disney first started drawing cartoons professionally in exchange for free haircuts.**

* Aspirin was the first drug offered as a water-soluble tablet.

Up to the age of about seven months, a baby can breathe and swallow at the same time.

In order for a deck of cards to be mixed up enough to play with properly, it should be shuffled at least seven times.

* Van Gogh didn't begin to draw until the age of 27.

Japanese researchers have calculated pi to 1.2411 trillion places.

* Transsexuals are allowed to compete in the Olympics.

The average person speaks at 125 to 150 words a minute.

* The average bank robbery yields £2,302.

* In an atom, the electron weighs 1/2000th the weight of a proton.

Japan is the largest exporter of frogs' legs.

* The girls of the Tiwi tribe in the South Pacific are married at birth.

* Going all 12 rounds in a heavyweight boxing match is the equivalent of getting hit on the head with a plank of wood more than 180 times.

* The metre was originally defined as one ten-millionth of the distance from the equator to the pole.

* When McDonald's opened its first restaurant in Kuwait, the drive-thru line was seven miles long.

* 4 October 2004 was the first day since 1999 that no one was shot in Chicago.

* The *USS Nautilus*, the world's first nuclear submarine, was also the first ship to cross the North Pole.

* The shortest sentence in the English language is "Go!"

* Between 1916 and 1918, the Grand National took place at Gatwick racecourse and not Aintree.

* The nine warmest years on record have all occurred since 1990.

Alfred Hitchcock did not have a bellybutton.

* The human stomach can distend to four litres. Impressive, compared to its resting volume of just 1.5 litres.

* The average smell weighs 760 nanograms.

* If an Amish man has a beard, he's married.

* Coldplay's Chris Martin's great-great-grandfather, William Willett, introduced the idea of putting the clocks forward one hour in spring, to create British Summertime.

```
The instrument used in shoe
shops to measure feet is
called the Brannock device.
```

* The oldest known vegetable is the pea.

* To strengthen a Damascus sword in ancient Syria, it was plunged into a slave.

* A dog is unable to hear the lowest key on a piano.

* A coward was originally a boy who looked after cows.

* The model ape used in the 1933 film *King Kong* stood only 18in tall.

* Americans – who account for just five per cent of the world's population – own one quarter of Earth's 530 million passenger cars.

* **As a result of California's three-strike policy, a man named Santos Reyes is serving 26 years for cheating on a driver's licence exam.**

* Libya is the only country with a single-coloured flag.

* **The first time women and men used separate toilets was in 1749 at a Parisian ball.**

* At 90 degrees below zero, your breath will freeze in mid-air and fall to the ground.

The Venus flytrap can eat a cheeseburger.

* **Women are twice as likely as men to have panic attacks.**

* An avalanche accelerates from 0–80mph in five seconds.

* **Vision requires more brainpower than any of the other four senses.**

* The average person goes to the toilet 2,500 times a year.

* **Paleoscatology is the study of fossilised turds.**

* There are twice as many left-handed men as there are left-handed women.

* **Schizophrenics hardly ever yawn.**

* Devon is the only county in Great Britain to have two coasts.

* **The Merseyside derby was first held in 1894.**

```
Parts of the Bible have been
translated into Klingon.
```

* In Albania, nodding your head means "no" and shaking it means "yes".

The most venomous of all snakes, the Inland Taipan, has enough venom to kill more than 200,000 mice.

* A commercial aeroplane will be airborne for approximately 14 hours per day and taxi 250,000 miles during its lifespan.

* Your mouth produces 1.8 pints of saliva every day.

* There are five trillion trillion atoms in one pound of iron.

* Camel milk doesn't curdle.

* The sun gives off enough energy in one second to power the entire USA for nine million years.

✳ If you stand with your eyes six feet above the surface of the ocean, the horizon will be about three miles away.

✳ **It would take around seven billion particles of fog to completely fill a teaspoon.**

✳ The tip of a 1cm-long hour hand on a wristwatch travels at exactly 0.00000275mph.

Pineapples do not ripen after they have been picked.

✳ **Approximately 17 per cent of humans are left-handed.**

✳ In similar volumes, printer cartridge ink is more expensive than rocket fuel.

✳ **In the 10th century, the Grand Vizier of Persia took his library wherever he went – 117,000 volumes carried in alphabetical order by more than 400 camels.**

* Brit Paul Hunn set the world record for the loudest burp with a 118.1-decibel belch – louder than a jet taking off 200 feet away (117 decibels).

```
The Taj Mahal was scheduled
to be torn down in the 1830s.
```

* **Desktop diva Danni Ashe is the most downloaded woman in internet history – with more than a billion downloads. Nerd fact: on a daily basis, Danni.com uses more bandwidth than all of Central America.**

* Every year in the UK, you run a one in 30,589,556 chance of being killed by "the ignition or the melting of your nightwear".

* **Kentucky law states that citizens must bathe once a year.**

* Keen to make a buck or two, the Canadian Mounted Police Force sold the rights to their image to Walt Disney.

* "Robot" comes from the Czech word "robota", meaning "forced labour".

* The first video game ever was developed by the US government in 1958. Its name, rather appallingly, was *Tennis For Two*.

A total of 35 professional footballers have been jailed since 1965.

* President Andrew Jackson's pet parrot was ejected from his 1845 funeral... for swearing.

* Around 6.3 per cent of sleepers have been rudely awakened by the "sweatiness" of their partner.

* There are lyrics to the theme song from *Star Trek*. But they're rubbish, starting with, "Beyond the rim of the starlight...".

* Killer Donald Webb, 73, has been on the FBI's Most-Wanted list for 24 years.

* In 2003, 50 Cent bought an 18-bedroom mansion in Connecticut, USA. The vendor was one Mike Tyson.

* Each hour, 32 women around the globe have breast implants. Just 17 an hour plump for a reduction.

* Cleopatra wrote a book on cosmetics. One of the ingredients was burnt mice.

Ducks only lay eggs in the early morning.

* At any one time, 19 million light bulbs need to be changed in the UK.

* There are currently 22,000 Humvees operating in Iraq. When the war began, just 235 were in service.

* Ice cream cones were first served at the 1904 World's Fair in St Louis.

* Norwich is the eBay capital of Britain.

* Only 30 per cent of humans can flare their nostrils. Try it.

* **An eagle can kill a wild deer... and fly away with it.**

* A human being loses between 40 to 100 strands of hair each day.

* **When you stub your toe, your brain registers pain in a 50th of a second.**

* The most common disease in the world is tooth decay.

```
Albino crabs are the
rarest albino
creatures.
```

* **Chap-loving chaps beware: there are no public toilets in Peru.**

* You inhale about 700,000 of your own skin flakes each day.

* Both the vagina and the eye are self-cleaning organs.

* While sleeping, one man in eight snores and one in ten grinds his teeth.

```
The Great Sphinx was carved
from a knoll left from the
quarrying of stone for
the Great Pyramid.
```

* It's harder to tell a convincing lie to someone you find sexually attractive.

* Anthropologists know of no human society whose children don't play hide and seek.

* La Paz in Bolivia is so high above sea level, there is barely enough oxygen in the air to support a fire.

* In China, it is against the law to save a drowning person. Why? You might be interfering with his or her fate.

* **Steve McQueen was on Charles Manson's murder hit list.**

* In the UK, you can be convicted for a criminal offence once you reach ten years old.

* **If current incarceration rates remain unchanged in the US, an estimated one in every nine men will serve time in prison.**

* Apple has sold more than ten million iPods since their debut in 2001.

* **The northern fur seal has more mates each year than any other mammal. The average male will mate with between 40 and 60 females each season.**

None of the Beatles knew how to read music.

* "The Great National Temperance Beverage" was a slogan for Coca-Cola in 1906.

* **A healthy bladder can hold up to two cups of urine comfortably for five hours.**

* Spanish doubloons were legal tender in the US until 1857.

* **The average person produces one to three pints of gas a day.**

```
Snickers is the best-selling
chocolate bar in both Russia
and the US.
```

* There is an official barbed wire museum in McLean, Texas, called the Devil's Rope Museum.

* **To be classified as sterling, an object must contain at least 92.5 per cent silver.**

* A cough releases an explosive charge of air that moves at speeds of up to 100mph.

* **Jeremy Clarkson's father-in-law won the VC.**

* One is the only number with its letters in reverse alphabetical order.

* **Nerve impulses travel through your body at over 250mph.**

* The Pacific Ocean covers 28 per cent of the Earth's surface.

* **In medieval times, Welsh mercenary bowmen wore one shoe at a time.**

```
The Queen Mary 2
passenger liner is
147 feet longer
than the Eiffel Tower is tall.
```

* Shell constitutes 12 per cent of an egg's weight.

* **Birmingham has 22 more miles of canal than Venice.**

* Airbags deploy at 200 miles per hour.

* **The Coca-Cola Company is the largest consumer of vanilla in the world.**

* More redheads are born in Scotland than in any other part of the world.

Wearing headphones for just an hour will increase the bacteria in your ear by 700 times.

* **The kiwi is the only bird with nostrils at the end of its bill. Somewhat unsurprisingly, it's also the only bird that can hunt by smell.**

* An impressive 28 per cent of Africa is wilderness.

* **Alfred Nobel invented dynamite. His father, Emmanuel, invented plywood.**

* Marlon Brando's occupation on his passport read "shepherd".

* **One in every eight romances between boss and secretary ends in marriage.**

* Frosties' Tony the Tiger will be 55 in 2007.

* **Condors can fly ten miles without flapping their wings.**

* The Putumayo River tribes of the Amazon would only eat captives after having an eight-day beer festival.

* **There are 1,800 known species of flea.**

* Every year, 250,000 people die after being exposed to pesticides.

```
Artist Leonardo da Vinci
invented scissors.
```

* **In the water? Watch yourself. Sharks will continue to attack even when disembowelled.**

* In 1971, Nike purchased the swoosh logo from a design student. It paid £20.

* In the US, 200,000,000 gallons of toilet water are flushed every hour.

* Shrimp swim backwards.

Martin Cooper, an engineer with Motorola, made the first mobile phone call on 3 April 1973.

* Illegible handwriting is known as "griffonage".

* During the First Crusade, a band of religious hysterics marched behind a goose they believed was filled with the Holy Spirit.

* Oak trees do not produce acorns until they are at least 50 years old.

* Of all international phone calls, 85 per cent are conducted in English.

* In the vast majority of languages, the word for "mother" begins with the letter "m".

✳ There's an average of 178 sesame seeds in a Big Mac bun.

✳ **About 75 per cent of people in the US live on two per cent of the land.**

Penguins can change salt water into fresh water.

✳ If you played all of the Beatles' singles and albums that came out between 1962 and 1970 back-to-back, it would only take ten hours and 33 minutes.

✳ **On Mercury, the sun seems two-and-a-half times larger than it appears on Earth.**

✳ It has been calculated that in the last 3,500 years, there have only been 230 years of peace throughout the civilised world.

✳ **The Earth's revolution time increases .0001 seconds annually.**

* Lord Byron's body is buried in England, but his lungs are buried in Greece.

* **One third of all cancers are sun-related.**

* Diet Coke was invented in 1982.

* **A human sperm is only 0.06mm long.**

* Popeye was 5ft 6ins tall.

* **Johann Sebastian Bach once walked 230 miles... simply to hear the organist at Lubeck in Germany.**

* In ten years, the average mattress doubles in weight thanks to waste matter from bed bugs and slumbering humans.

The Macadamia nut has the hardest shell of all nuts.

* **There are more than 33,000 radio stations in the world.**

* The world record for carrying a milk bottle on a human head is 24 miles.

* **Almonds are the most popular nuts in the world.**

```
A koala will only eat
six of the 500 species
of eucalyptus leaves in
existence.
```

* The average talker sprays about 300 microscopic saliva droplets per minute – 2.5 droplets per word.

* **Fido means "faithful" in Latin.**

* The longest straight section of railway in the world (298.75 miles) is on the Nullarbor Plain in Southern Australia.

* **At full speed, a space shuttle would be able to fly from New York to Los Angeles in just ten minutes.**

* The odds of dying while in the bath are one in a million.

* **It costs more to buy a car today than it cost Christopher Columbus to equip and undertake three voyages to the New World.**

* Rats can distinguish between languages.

```
A grizzly bear can run 100 yards
in 4.3 seconds.
```

* **Aluminium is strong enough to support 90,000 pounds per square inch.**

* Karate originated in India.

* **World War II involved more than 57 countries.**

* One out of four people don't know what their astrological sign is.

* **The harmonica is the world's most popular instrument.**

* A portable PC on your lap can raise the temperature of your testicles almost six degrees an hour. It only takes a two-degree raise to reduce sperm count.

* **The Soviet *Sukhoi-34* was the first strike fighter with a toilet in it.**

* The armhole in clothing is called an "armsaye".

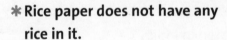

```
The Chinese invented
the wheelbarrow.
```

* **Rice paper does not have any rice in it.**

* Driving at 75 miles per hour, it would take 258 days to drive around one of Saturn's rings.

* **It takes a plastic container 50,000 years to begin decomposition.**

✳ Bees do not have ears.

✳ **Each year, a tonne of cement is poured for each man, woman and child in the world.**

At birth, a panda bear is smaller than a mouse.

✳ 888,000 credit cards in circulation have incorrect cardholder information on their magnetic strips.

✳ **Since the Gambino crime family was founded in the US, five of its 16 bosses (31 per cent) have been murdered.**

✳ Three teaspoons make up one tablespoon.

✳ **It is legal to marry a dead person in France.**

✳ There are 42 dots on a pair of dice.

✳ **Japan's currency – the yen – is the most difficult to counterfeit.**

* Around 60 per cent of circulating American currency (around $370billion) is held outside the USA.

* **Astronauts in orbit around the Earth can see the wake left by ships.**

* Bats, monkeys and shrews all have penis bones.

* **Iron nails cannot be used in oak. The acid in the wood corrodes them.**

```
CDs were developed by
Philips and Sony in
1980.
```

* George W Bush was a cheerleader in school.

* **The last word in the Bible is... Amen.**

* The bowling ball was invented in 1862.

* **There are 412 doors in the White House.**

* Alexander Graham Bell, inventor of the telephone, never phoned his wife or mother, as both were deaf.

* **The word "pornography" comes from the Greek phrase meaning "the writings of prostitutes".**

The average American consumes enough caffeine in one year to kill a horse.

* Eighty-five per cent of every Volvo is recyclable.

* **There are 529 positions in the *Kama Sutra*.**

* The original Guinness brewery in Dublin has a 6,000-year lease.

* **The circumference of the smallest star in Orion's Belt is larger than the Earth's path around the sun.**

* $203million (£111.1million) is spent on barbed wire each year in the US.

* **One species of antelope, the sitatunga, can sleep underwater.**

* The Old English word for sneeze is "fneosan".

* **The average salary in the UK is £24,440.**

```
Gorillas sleep for up
to 14 hours every day.
```

* A top freestyle swimmer can achieve a maximum speed of 4mph.

* **In medieval England, people quite often drank beer with their breakfast.**

* When the *Titanic* sank, there was 7,500lb of ham on board.

* **Sony was originally called "Totsuken".**

* Matt Damon has an indoor basketball court in his New York loft apartment.

Every hour, the Church of Scientology recruits 129 people.

* **When born, the brown myotis bat's young are the equivalent size to a woman giving birth to a 30lb baby.**

* After the Popeye comic strip started in 1931, spinach consumption in the US increased by 33 per cent.

* **Traffic lights were first used in 1868. That's 18 years before the first car was invented.**

* It takes 11 truckloads of wood to make a funeral pyre for an adult elephant.

* **Yak milk is pink.**

* A can of Diet Coke will float in water, while a can of Classic Coke sinks.

* **China's Beijing Duck Restaurant can seat 9,000 people at one time.**

* The average cow releases 600 litres of methane per day.

* **In 1955, one-third of all watches sold were made by Timex.**

Before football referees started using whistles in 1878, they used to rely on waving a handkerchief.

* The Statue of Liberty's mouth is three feet wide.

* **Playing cards in India are round.**

* Spat-out food is called chanking.

* **2,488,200 books will be shipped in the next 12 months with the wrong cover.**

* Kleenex tissues were originally used as filters in gas masks.

* **If you were to light a match in a space shuttle, the flame would be spherical.**

* Eagles can live in captivity for up to 46 years.

* **Australia is the easiest continent to defend in the game of Risk.**

* A deltiologist collects postcards.

```
Sterile female ants are the
ones that do all the work.
```

* **Table salt is the only commodity that hasn't risen dramatically in price in the past 150 years.**

* Dogs and cats consume over £7billion worth of pet food a year in the UK.

* **Scooby Doo's real first name is Scoobert.**

* The average sumo wrestler weighs about 20 stone.

* **The longest game of Monopoly in a bath lasted 99 hours.**

* In the '40s, the Bich pen was changed to Bic in case Americans pronounced it "Bitch".

* **In the summer, walnuts get a tan.**

* Honey is used as a centre for golf balls and in antifreeze mixtures.

* **The red mullet only turns red after death.**

* At the Lego mould factories, five-thousandths of a millimetre is the level of accuracy.

```
More bullets were fired in
Starship Troopers than in any
other movie.
```

* **Diamond dust is black.**

Spain literally means
"the land of rabbits".

* In 1981, a man had a heart attack after playing the game Beserk – video gaming's only known fatality.

* **The Slinky, the spring toy, is sold on every continent of the world, except Antarctica.**

* Walt Disney's autograph bears no resemblance to the famous Disney logo.

* **A jumbo jet uses 4,000 gallons of fuel to take off.**

* A manned rocket can now reach the moon in less time than it once took a stagecoach to travel the length of England.

* **There are 3,900 islands in Japan.**

* The external tank on the space shuttle is never painted.

* **The first atomic bomb exploded at Trinity Site, New Mexico, on 16 July 1945.**

* Pluto, the astrological sign for death, was directly above Dallas, Texas, when JFK was born.

* **Stainless steel was discovered by accident in 1913.**

* The Roman emperor Caligula is said to have made his horse a senator.

* **In English gambling dens, people were employed to swallow the dice if police arrived.**

* Al Capone's brother was a town sheriff.

```
There are three golf balls
sitting on the moon.
```

* **The Siberian larch accounts for more than 20 per cent of all the world's trees.**

* The radioactive substance Americanium-241 is used in many smoke detectors.

* **Prior to World War II, when the decision was taken to post guards at the fence, anyone could walk right up to the front door of the White House.**

* Kodak is the world's largest user of silver.

```
In ancient Greece, women
counted their age from the
date they were married.
```

* **The foundations of most European cathedrals go down 50 feet.**

* The shockwave from a nitroglycerine explosion travels at 17,000 miles per hour.

* **Most burglaries occur in winter.**

* Big Bird is 8ft 2ins tall.

* **Eskimos never gamble.**

* There are more statues of Joan of Arc in the world than of anyone else. France alone has about 40,000 of them.

The strength of early lasers was measured in Gillettes — the number of razor blades the laser could cut through.

* **Sunbeams that shine down through clouds are called crepuscular rays.**

* The Wright brothers' first plane was called *The Bird Of Prey*.

* **The average life of a nuclear power plant is 40 years.**

* Saint Stephen is the patron saint of bricklayers.

* **A necropsy is an autopsy on animals.**

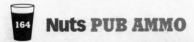

* In George Bush's home state of Texas, only one in four children graduate.

* **A full moon is nine times brighter than a half moon.**

* The smallest unit of time is the yoctosecond. It's one septillionth of a second.

* **The optimum depth of water in a birdbath is two-and-a-half inches.**

* Toads only eat moving prey.

```
Toronto was the first city
in the world to have a
computerised traffic
signal system.
```

* **The two hottest months at the equator are March and September.**

* There are micro-organisms on earth that can only live in the absence of oxygen.

* Orchids are grown from seeds so small that it would take 30,000 to weigh as much as one grain of wheat.

* India has the largest stock of privately hoarded gold.

* The Venus flytrap takes half a second to shut on its prey.

* There are 2,000,000 different combinations of sandwich that can be created from a Subway menu.

* It takes 25 muscles to swallow.

* The weight of crisps eaten each year by Americans is six times more than that of the *Titanic*.

```
If you attempted to count the
stars in a galaxy at a rate of
one every second, it would
take around 3,000 years to
count them all.
```

* **A fully loaded standard army issue M16 weighs less than an Xbox console.**

* The Mona Lisa was stolen from the Louvre in Paris in August 1911.

It takes one 15-to 20-year-old tree to produce 700 brown paper bags.

* **Director William Friedkin edited *The Exorcist* in a building situated at 666 Fifth Avenue, New York.**

* At room temperature, air molecules travel at the speed of a rifle bullet.

* **The first computer ever made was called ENIAC.**

* Before 1850, golf balls were made of leather and stuffed with feathers.

* **The most popular contact lens colour is blue.**

* The entire cost of building the Empire State Building was £23,157,166.

* **The royal house of Saudi Arabia has close to 10,000 princes and princesses.**

Popeye has four nephews.
They're called Poopeye, Pupeye,
Pipeye and Peepeye.

* The first western consumer product sold in the old Soviet Union was Pepsi.

* **Ivanov is the most common Russian surname.**

* The English word "magic" comes from a mysterious priestly clan from Persia (now Iran) called the Magi.

* **The average bank cashier loses £175 a year.**

* German is considered the sister language of English.

* Martin van Buren, the eighth American president, was the first not to have been born a British subject.

* Elvis' name is spelt incorrectly on his grave. It reads "Aaron", not "Aron" as he was christened.

* Germany's autobahns are 27 inches thick.

* Blueberries are actually purple in colour.

A large flawless emerald is worth more than a similarly large flawless diamond.

* Ancient China traded with imperial Rome, but the Chinese and Romans never met.

* There are over 1,000 examples of cockney rhyming slang.

* Use of the cat-o'-nine-tails was finally suspended in the Royal Navy in 1879.

* A cat called Towser, owned by the Glenturret Distillery in Scotland, is reported to have killed an average of three mice a day for every day of her adult life, giving her an estimated kill count of 28,899 mice.

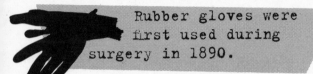

Rubber gloves were first used during surgery in 1890.

* The first oil well in modern times was just 21 metres deep.

* F1 magnate Bernie Ecclestone is worth £2.3billion.

* Every year more than 100,000 jury trials are held in US courts – 90 per cent of the world total.

* According to the Bible (Genesis 1:20–22), the chicken came before the egg.

* Sweden made bestiality legal in 1944.

* The highest motorway in England is the M62 from Liverpool to Hull.

* **The shortest English word with the letters A, B, C, D, E and F is "feedback".**

* The fear of being stared at is called ophthalmophobia.

* **The strip club industry in the US rakes in $15billion (£8.5billion) each year.**

* More people are allergic to cow's milk than any other food.

* **The first diesel engine ran on peanut oil.**

The last reported snowfall in LA was 8 February 1989.

* Napoleon's real height was 5ft 7ins.

* **The real name of Shaggy, of *Scooby Doo* fame, is Norville.**

* Electricity doesn't move through a wire, but through a field around the wire.

> "Vodka" is Russian for "little water".

* **Cockroaches break wind every 15 minutes.**

* There are 46 miles of nerves in the human body.

* **There is a city called Rome on every continent.**

* It takes approximately 69,000 venom extractions from the coral snake to fill a pint glass.

* **Earth actually has two moons. Cruithne, not discovered until 1986, only orbits the Earth every 780 years or so.**

* The "G" in G-string stands for "groin".

* Ten per cent of the national income of Liechtenstein comes from the sale of stamps.

* The oldest captive bear in the world is 32 years old.

* Five baseball gloves can be made from one cow.

* Avocado gets its name from the Aztec word for testicle.

```
The lower leg, from the knee
down, constitutes 15 per cent of
a body's weight.
```

* There are 134 two-letter words in the English language.

* The average yawn lasts six seconds.

* The heart beats faster during a heated argument than it does during sex.

* Dogs are capable of understanding 40 to 50 verbal expressions.

* **America's first president, George Washington, earned a salary of £25,000.**

* The medical term for earwax is cerumen.

To protect the secret of their "Original Recipe", KFC use two separate companies to blend the herbs and spices so that neither ever has the complete recipe.

* **The first email was sent over the internet in 1971.**

* You can find a bunny hidden on every cover of *Playboy* magazine.

* **A person can't taste food unless it's mixed with saliva.**

* The flu vaccination is made from chicken embryos.

* A single mating pair of house flies can generate as many as 325,923,200,000,000 offspring in one summer.

* Your heart rate can rise as much as 30 per cent during a yawn.

* Forty-one per cent of Europeans speak English as a second language.

* The first national anthem was *God Save The King*, first performed in public in 1745.

In Australia, Burger King is called Hungry Jack's.

* Along the moon's equator, dawn arrives at only 10mph – slow enough for a man on a bicycle to keep up with it.

* The "Luther Burger", a bacon cheeseburger served on a Krispy Kreme doughnut bun, named after R&B singer Luther Vandross, weighs in at 828 calories.

✳ **A person swallows approximately 295 times while eating dinner.**

Belle laide is a French phrase, translated as "beautiful-ugly", and refers to a woman who is not beautiful but is somehow attractive.

✳ It takes six months to build a Rolls-Royce Camargue and 13 hours to build a Toyota Corolla.

✳ **50 Cent has become the first artist since the Beatles to hold four positions in the US Top 10 at the same time.**

✳ The roof of Beijing's new airport will cover 80 acres.

✳ **Only one per cent of British roads are motorways, but they carry 20 per cent of the traffic.**

* Hurricanes get their names from Huracan, a West Indian god of storms.

* **On just one square inch of your skin, there are 20 million microscopic organisms.**

* One in 500 humans has one blue eye and one brown eye.

* **There is no iced tea in a Long Island Iced Tea.**

The first "space wedding" was between astronaut Yuri Malenchenko, aboard the International Space Station, and Ekaterina Dmitriev, who was in Texas.

* Caligynephobia is the fear of beautiful women.

* **Giraffes, camels and cats are the only animals that walk by moving both their left feet, then both their right feet.**

* Of all the senses, smell is most closely linked to memory.

* **We began officially naming tropical storms and hurricanes in 1953. In 1979, male names were added to the list.**

According to *Smithsonian* magazine, fear of the number 13 costs Yanks $1billion per year in absenteeism and train and plane cancellations on the 13th of the month.

* Twenty-two per cent of all restaurant meals include French fries.

* **At 151, Indonesia has more active volcanoes than any other country.**

* Women make up 49 per cent of the world's population.

* **There are more than 30,000 diets on public record.**

* If you chew aluminium foil, it reacts with saliva and fillings to form a tiny battery – causing a tiny electric shock.

* **In 2004, for the fifth year in a row, trucks outsold cars in the US.**

* Identical twins do not have identical fingerprints.

* **Eighty per cent of the world's hard drives have personal photos on them.**

```
Tonka trucks were named
after Lake Minnetonka in
Minnesota.
```

* A wolf's odour-detecting ability is 100 times greater than man's.

* **There's a special section in the brain reserved for the thumb that's separate from the area that controls the fingers.**

* The moon is actually moving away from Earth at a rate of 1.5 inches per year.

* **The average adult loses 540 calories with every litre of sweat.**

In Las Vegas, it's illegal to pawn your dentures.

* There are 15,000 different kinds of rice.

* **A pound of crisps costs almost 200 times more than a pound of potatoes.**

* The Sahara Desert's total land mass is approximately 3,565,565 square miles – an area as large as Europe.

* **The United States Mint once considered producing doughnut-shaped coins.**

* Ron Jeremy holds the record for "most appearances (1,750) in adult films" in the *Guinness Book Of World Records*.

* **Air conditioning units use 98 per cent more energy than ceiling fans.**

* A house fly can change direction in mid-air in 30 milliseconds.

* **"Almost" is the longest word in the English language with all the letters in alphabetical order.**

* A meteor has only destroyed one satellite, the European Space Agency's *Olympus* in 1993.

* **Basketball was invented in 1891.**

* A "face-off" in hockey was initially called a "puck-off", but was changed for obvious reasons.

Because he hates product placement in films, Quentin Tarantino uses fictional cigarette brand Red Apple and defunct cereal Fruit Brute in his movies.

* **Chocolate manufacturers use 40 per cent of the world's almonds.**

* Diamond substitute Cubic Zirconia is 55 per cent heavier than real diamond.

* **Bubblegum contains rubber.**

One penny doubled every day becomes over five million pounds in just 30 days.

* If you earn £20,000 per year, one minute of your time is worth just over 17 pence.

* **Camel meat is considered unclean according to the Bible.**

* Ten books on a shelf can be arranged in 3,628,800 different ways.

* **Badminton is the world's fastest racquet sport, with smashes reaching speeds up to 206mph.**

* A cubic yard of air weighs about 2lb at sea level.

* **Every year, £600,000 goes unclaimed due to betting slips that have been lost or not checked.**

* The act of snapping your fingers is called a fillip.

* **The Snickers bar was named after a horse.**

```
The smartest dogs are the
Jack Russell terrier and
Scottish Border collie.
The dumbest is the
Afghan hound.
```

* Purple is considered a majestic colour because it was a sign of great rank in ancient Rome.

* **Handshakes transmit viruses seven times more effectively than sneezes do.**

* The US share of the world music market is 31.3 per cent.

* **A married man is four times more likely to die during sex if his partner isn't his wife.**

* Contrary to popular belief, hair does not grow back darker and thicker after it has been shaved.

The female lion does more than 90 per cent of the hunting.

* **The time spent deleting spam emails costs US businesses $21.6billion (£11.7billion) annually.**

* A barking dog is not usually a sign of aggressive behaviour – it's the silent, snarling or growling dog that is actually most dangerous.

* **An octopus' testicles are in its head.**

* It takes one day to get a divorce in the Dominican Republic.

* **The word "hallelujah" is common to all languages.**

* Koalas, iguanas and Komodo dragons all have forked penises.

* **The estimated number of M&Ms sold each day in the US is 200,000,000.**

* In May 1991, an abused goat killed its owner.

* **After the release of *The Deer Hunter*, press reports claimed there had been 25 deaths from people imitating the Russian roulette scene.**

Impotence is grounds for divorce in 24 US states.

* In the Middle Ages, chicken soup was believed to be an aphrodisiac.

* Jodie Foster was George Lucas' second option for Princess Leia in *Star Wars*.

Women purchase 93 per cent of all greeting cards.

* Not all our taste buds are on our tongue; about ten per cent are on the palate and the cheeks.

* September, October, November, and December should be the 7th, 8th, 9th and 10th months respectively, but Julius Caesar rearranged the calendar to start with January instead of March.

* A battologist is someone who pointlessly repeats themselves.

* Billboards are banned in Alaska and Hawaii.

* In 1916, 55 per cent of the cars in the world were Model T Fords, a record never beaten.

* The colder the room you sleep in, the better the chances you'll have a bad dream.

* The world's highest waterfall is Angel Falls in Venezuela, which drops 3,212 feet.

* In the past 55 years, 480 fugitives have appeared on the FBI's 10 Most Wanted List.

* Every hour, 799 Cuban cigars are illegally imported into America.

* The computing power of the chip in a musical birthday card is greater than that owned by the combined Allied forces in WWII.

The world's deadliest recorded earthquake occurred in 1557 in central China, killing 830,000.

* A quidnunc is a person who is eager to know the latest news and gossip.

* Twenty-four per cent of M&Ms in a bag are blue, the highest percentage of any colour.

* All Arabian horses can be traced back to one of three stallions: the Byerly Turk, the Darley Arabian or the Godolphin Barb.

The French kiss is so called because it was used in the Brittany village of Pays de Mont as a substitute for sex because the population was growing too fast.

* Lyre birds can imitate any sound they hear, from a car alarm to an electric chainsaw.

* The sitcom *Mork & Mindy* was actually a spin-off of *Happy Days*.

* The two-hour pilot of *Lost* cost £5.6 million to film.

Odontophobia is the fear of teeth.

* James Gandolfini earned $13million for the fifth season of *The Sopranos* – $1million per episode.

* **In Rochester, Michigan, the law states that anyone bathing in public must have their bathing suit inspected by a police officer.**

* Every day, American businesses use enough paper to circle the Earth's equator more than 20 times.

* **The right lung takes in more air than the left.**

* More people die of allergic reactions to strawberries in a year than from shark attacks.

* **The maximum score on an arcade Pac-Man is 3,333,360.**

* The world record for rocking non-stop in a rocking chair is 480 hours, held by Dennis Easterling of Atlanta, Georgia.

* **All the pet hamsters in the world are descended from one female wild golden hamster found with a litter of 12 young in Syria in 1930.**

* It was once law in France that children's names had to be taken from an official government list.

According to the National Violence Against Women Survey, approximately 370,000 men are stalked each year.